Little Mitchie

LET'S LOOK INSIDE A CRUISE SHIP

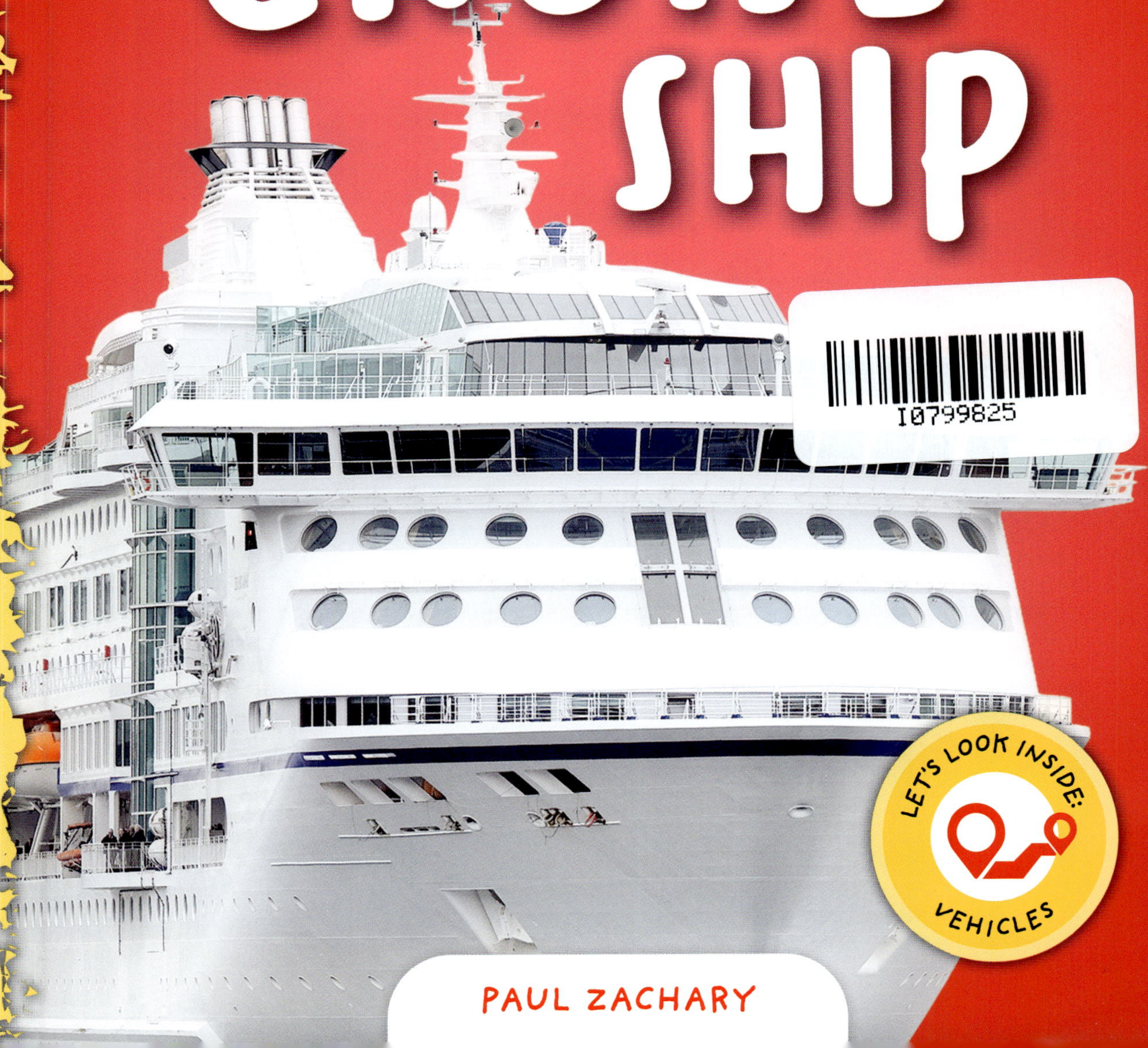

LET'S LOOK INSIDE: VEHICLES

PAUL ZACHARY

CREATING YOUNG NONFICTION READERS

Little Mitchie books spark curiosity and support early nonfiction reading for students in Grades 2-3. Designed to build vocabulary, support second language learners, and prepare readers for middle-grade content, each book includes helpful tips for parents and educators to build confidence and deepen understanding of the world.

TIPS FOR READING NONFICTION WITH BEGINNING READERS

Talk about Nonfiction

Begin by explaining that nonfiction books give us information that is true. The book will be organized around a specific topic or idea, and we may learn new facts through reading.

Look at the Parts

Most nonfiction books have helpful features. Our *Little Mitchie* titles include color photographs and graphic aids, a table of contents, a glossary, and an index. Share the purpose of these features with your reader.

Color Photos and Graphic Aids

A lot of information can be found by "reading" photos, charts, maps, and other graphic aids found within nonfiction texts. Help your reader learn more about the different ways information can be displayed.

Table of Contents

Located at the front of the book, this list shows the big ideas within the text and the page numbers where they can be found.

Glossary

Located at the back of the book, the glossary defines key words and phrases that are related to the topic. These words and phrases can be found in the text in colored type.

Index

Located at the back of the book, an index is an alphabetical list of topics and the page numbers where they can be found.

With a little help and guidance about reading nonfiction, you can feel good about introducing a young reader to the world of *Little Mitchie* nonfiction books.

Little Mitchie is an imprint of:

Mitchell Lane
PUBLISHERS

2001 SW 31st Avenue
Hallandale, FL 33009
mitchelllanepub.com

First Edition, 2027.

Author: Paul Zachary
Designer: Rhea Magaro
Editor: Tricia Hoffman

Library of Congress Cataloging-in-Publication Data
Title: Let's Look Inside a Cruise Ship / by Paul Zachary.

Description: Hallandale, FL :
Mitchell Lane Publishers, [2027]

Identifiers:
ISBN 979-8-89260-878-7 (library bound)
ISBN 979-8-90145-047-5 (paperback)
ISBN 979-8-89260-981-4 (eBook)

Library of Congress Control Number: 2026930301

Photo credits: Alamy: Danita Delimont 6; Royal Carribean: 8, 12, 15, 22; Shutterstock: Vereshchagin Dmitry, 3; Ceri Breeze, 20; Anton Watman, 9; Solarisys, 11; ER_09, 18; balipadma, 16; NAN728, 5

TABLE OF CONTENTS

Chapter One

AHOY THERE!

Look at that giant boat. It's a cruise ship! It is as tall as a building and as long as a train.

But what's inside this floating city? Let's climb aboard and explore!

We walk up the ramp and into the main lobby of the ship. Wow! We see shiny floors, twinkling lights, and a big glass elevator that goes up and down. There's music playing, people smiling, and the ocean sparkling just outside the windows.

We visit the **cabins** where people will sleep in cozy beds. There is a bathroom, a little desk, and a TV in each room. Some cabins even have balconies to see the ocean!

SHIP-SHAPE FACT

The world's biggest cruise ships can be longer than three football fields.

Chapter Two

LET'S EAT!

The dining rooms are huge, with white tablecloths covering hundreds of tables. This ship has a **buffet** with rows and rows of food. We can have pancakes, pizza, fruit, or ice cream! And we can eat as much as we want—as long as our parents say it's okay!

SHIP-SHAPE FACT

On a cruise ship, you can eat almost any time of the day.

FLOWRIDER

Chapter Three

FUN ON BOARD

Want to go for a swim? Let's head out to the pool **deck**! This ship has a swimming pool, a **splash zone**, and even twisty **water slides**. Kids laugh and swim while their parents relax on deck chairs, wearing sunglasses and big smiles.

After our pool time, we go inside again. This time, we head to the **theater**.

It's dark and quiet as the curtains rise. Then the music starts! Dancers spin, singers sing, and **magicians** make rabbits appear!

SHIP-SHAPE FACT

Some of the biggest cruise ships can carry more than 6,000 passengers and more than 2,000 crew members.

COSTA

Chapter Four

WOW, THERE'S MORE TO DO!

Now let's head to the kids' club. Here, we can play games, do crafts, and make new friends. There are blocks, coloring tables, and dress-up corners. Friendly crew members help everyone have fun and stay safe.

Downstairs, the ship has a gym, a spa, and even a tiny shopping mall. Passengers can buy a stuffed dolphin, souvenir T-shirts, or a captain's hat!

The next time we see a cruise ship on the water, we'll know it's not just a boat. It's a magical world floating on the waves!

A LOOK INSIDE

GLOSSARY

buffet (buh-fay) a meal where you can choose from lots of different foods and serve yourself

cabin (kab-in) a small room on a ship where people sleep

crew member (kroo mem-ber) a person who works on a ship to help passengers and keep everything running

deck (dek) a flat, open area on a ship where people can walk or swim

magicians (muh-jish-uhns) people who perform tricks that look like magic, often making objects appear or disappear

splash zone (splash zohn) an area with water fun, like fountains, sprinklers, or small pools for kids to play in

theater (thee-uh-ter) a room where people watch shows, music, dancing, or magic tricks

water slide (waw-ter slide) a twisty chute that slides into a pool

FURTHER READING

Carr, Aaron. *Cruise Ships.* Weigl Publishers, 2022.

Swan, Emma. *Cruise Ship Kid: Thief at Sea.* Usborne, 2025.

ON THE INTERNET

Cruise Ship Facts for Kids

https://kids.kiddle.co/Cruise_ship

Easy-to-read basics about what a cruise ship is, what life on board is like, and fun features like swimming pools and activities.

Ship

https://kids.britannica.com/kids/article/ship/390850

Britannica Kids explains the different types of ships and their uses.

INDEX